CUT

CUT

en medias res

CLAUDE MOORE

PARLYAREE
PRESS

Parlyaree Press
Atlanta, Georgia
www.parlyaree.com

Library of Congress Cataloging-in-Publication Data
Names: Moore, Claude, author.
Title: Cut: In Medias Res / Claude Moore
Description: First Edition | Atlanta : Parlyaree Press, 2025
Identifiers: LCCN: | ISBN 9781961206144 (paperback)
Subjects: LCGFT: Poetry
LC record available at https://lccn.loc.gov/

Design by Parlyaree Press

Front Cover/Title Typeface is Continuo by Delve Withrington from
Delve Fonts & Avenir designed by Adrian Frutiger and released by
Linotype GmbH. Glyphs from Espiritu, Cardo, Apple Symbols, and
LTC Fleurons.
Cover Imagery (Scissors) Licensed from Adobe.
Interior Text Typeface is Clarendon URW from URW Type Foundry.

Print ISBN: 978-1-961206-14-4
Ebook ISBN: 978-1-961206-15-1

To finding oneself in the middle of things.

An open wound.

The scar.

Table of Contents

Open.
Accept what enters in rhythmic lilt
A language of seduction where the ebb and flow
Mimic oceans under moons.

In altruism, you have agreed to take me on, knowing full well you are entering in the middle of things and may well full be burned by the process.

Will you be silent as my flames lick through the caverns of your body,

       search out depths in your navel,

             gaze a solemn history into your eyes?

You will receive a past you are not ready for. I can promise you that much. Too, maybe two or three moments of pleasure to match a broadened surface with the scars you will find in your exploration of me. Those things were pleasurable once too, I assure you. We can make them enjoyable again.

There is something sweet about existing in your periphery. I find it exhilarating how you pretend I am not there. A learned behavior, perhaps, on my part.

First, your ignorance. (Why do you ignore me so?)

Then, the othering.

Set me apart, delicate maybe, on a shelf far out of reach where you can just barely make out the colors of my flag. Tell me I am nothing. Then: when we meet in back alleys and bathrooms, be surprised I do not reveal my name. Marvel at my ability to turn your slight into eroticism. I'll take your anonymity, contain it. Raise it up the pole.

We planted in twos
Tiger lilies and hellebores; hydrangeas
With blossoms like confetti, beads
Of snapdragon, lavender, and
Tomatoes—so many tomatoes—
More than we could ever eat
We let them ripen on the vine

We planted in twos
As if we knew a flood was coming
Seeds sewn into the hems of our clothing
Hemlock and poppies
Witch's bane, rue, and pennyroyal
And other things we'd found or collected
Along the way knowing
They would sprout up
One day if we were to fall

We planted in twos
—Okay, sometimes threes, but who's counting—
To create a sense of place
One meant to last beyond
The two of us, planted
Like tiger lilies and hellebores
Into the well-trod earth

I found a bit of happiness, it's true
(Is this who I am now?)
Mixed, as it was, among the discarded words
Of our last conversation. The syllables
Which fell beatific within the un-
Pronounced letters, missing only you,
Like u had been there all along
Silent in the downbeat
When we both laughed into the night

What should we call it then? This—
Indulgence. This—
Craving.
Do we listen for the wording to appear on the wind?
The sound the echoes make from where
Our insides were hollowed out
Reverberate, sigh, rattle—again—
This unrelenting need for a language
To be invented. (Invent it then!)
We will say this to ourself. This—
Stumble. This—
Trip.
Stutter, a verbal slip, over the words
Silky and smooth and supple on our tongue.
(Delicious)
Heavy there and filling
An understatement if ever there was.
But we knew this already. This fault
Lined up at the edge of the cliff
Ready to sing.

GOLEM

Take soft light from my shoulders
Whittle it down like wood-stuffs
Sharp at the end of your pocketknife
And brighter still with every cut
Jab about until I am left in shape
Resembling someone honest (who? me?)
And kind (what? never!)
And open to a darkness I have not yet known

I am, in very much the sense that I will be and was, something of a Perseus, though I must confess this is purely conjectured etymology. For you see, I have saved no maidens from the sea, nor have I denied the gorgon of her snakes. Instead I have simply wasted. I have ravaged. I have destroyed. I have made a noun of these actions, all of them. Yes, I will be that.

Could I be, then, and now too perhaps, a misinterpretation? A single letter skewed with the flourish of a hand to become misread. Exchange an "l" for an "r" I say. Where Argos was Mycenae was Algos was Pain. All of this here in perpetuity. Yes, that is who I always was.

Call me firebrand. Place the word beneath my tongue, me into your kiln. Let me calcify, harden evermore until I am suitable for use. It is for you to decide, is it not, my purpose. If I am to be a vessel, I must be in the possession of some sort of strength. Have a mouth from which to pour. Me: the rapscallion, the agitator, the nonconformist. Burn me until I am to your liking or else done enough to discard.

This is true, also, from the other side. Though this notion of sides betrays me, I have felt it there as well. Piercing like spears beneath the ribcage. The molding of the clay until the golem is but one distinct message. No need for nuance or for parts that do not fit. They will celebrate my difference and suck it in, bite down, cleave it in two within the same breath. Do not nonconform like this, they will say. They will say it with a smile and a flame.

I can say whatever I want of my history on these

pages. Make it **tall & bold**, in *italics*, and
always slightly   askew. I can do
so because you have no option to respond.

(How exhilarating!!!)

It is to me then—and only me: where I am me and you
are also me—to create this dialogue—a liturgy really,
as you were also so devout—so we, the two of us, may
converse. Then, if you are to respond, aloud or with
the red of your pen in the margins, it can be a true
conversation. The type we always had. Where I said
my unchanging peace. And you said your own.

Take back your letters!
I demand it!
Here: they serve no purpose save for extraneous
ornament. I will close my eyes so I do not have to
listen.

Turn my head.

Take it on my back.

Y: How dare you write in such absurdities?!?

M: Am I no thing more than the inflections you place upon me? Do I exist beyond the page?

Y: I create you in my mind, and thus have created a monster. You must cease from being.

M: Is it not always the same story? You desire nothing more than my nonexistence.

Y: Afford me this then: Silence.

M: Ahhh, but I am silent. It is you who has decided when I scream.

Y: Scream then. Yell. Slice across the page.

M:

Y: So you shall not?

M: ...

Y: Speak!

M: I will do no such thing as I must wait for you to finish.

I am not so easily moved, it would seem, as our past has become. Yes, I see the space you have set aside for the evolution of language. It is true also that I see the disparity in what you are willing to report (*for I am willing to see it, you see*). The euphemism of adherence (*we mustn't queer the old view!*) to the words once used for protection. (*This is important! We must return to this later!*) The nom de plume like my own. The tomboy hair and the dandy's scarf collection. The flat shared with the best friend along the River Styx. The two (*too?*) token fare for passage. This, I say to you now: I may evolve as the language we have evolves. I may change as swiftly as your consonants. I will be my own form of slang, invent my own way of being. So that what I call me then can become what you will call me later. Yes, I will even take your slurs, roll them around in my mouth, and have them be celebrated. Yet, because I am a communal soul, I will now seek to commune with you with the only words you know.

Y: How dare you redefine what that means?!?

M: I dare not. I am simply expanding its meaning to you.

DEVOUT CREATIONS

You call yourself "devout."

Surely it is not so difficult, then, for you to see me through the eyes of your:

1) **God** - Wherein a capitalization has occurred. An all-seeing, all-knowing omnipotence (redundant, really, as it were) which may encompass me in creation. Therein I must, too, be holy. Should I not be? For certainly your God is not capable of divining such evils. ("My God is capable of all things," you say. "My God should always be not not capable." To which I respond: Then your God is surely capable of me.)

2) **god(s)** - That very pluralization of being—the name(s) you give the elements—should course as strongly through me as through you. Each river and subsidiary flowing into one another and out, out, out to the vastness of oceans.

3) **love** - Yes, love. For I love as strongly as you. And where you still see yours plainly—in texts and films and songs with the appropriate pronouns—I too will see mine. It is coded, but I have learned to carry my own cipher within the optical nerve.

4) **youth** - For mine is an old love, older even than my being. It seeps through history in the way an idea drips blood: hardens and scabs when exposed. So here we are: you, pluralized (like god), hardened and lisping at the end: exposed.

Quick! Apply your salve.
Condition the skin not to rip with every word you
       speak against me.
Tell me you: are sorry/are sincere/are changed.
Tell me you:
       do not include me (heavens, no!) in your
       othered.
Wallow there. Fingers thick with vaseline.
Spread until it hurts
No more in your thoughts. The ointment was
for your comfort after all. To blur the lens
so you would not need to watch me bleed.

You said * move * and my body wavered omnidirectionally. I wanted to take up all of the space you could have wanted me in. I would do that for you, you know. Pull myself apart to be *more* and *less* simultaneously. If that was what you wanted. Is it what you want?

You need a *then* and a *now* to exist, yet I am forever. I am forever focused on a future in which we * move * in an outward motion, spreading like petals opened in the spring, like winged flight before winter. I can be what I am in all of those places, be what you want me to be to notice the vagrancy of my body.

I spread and I spread and I spread and you say,

"See!

There!"

You think you have captured me.

On the stoop

An extra finger of ash

Waiting to fall, and you

Still, sparkling

Glitter on your brow, in your hair

On the part of your chest still seen since

You put your shirt back on say

"You're going to lose it."

We walked fifteen blocks

On two streets

Neighborhoods filled

With like-minds chanting

Caged bird songs

Of freedom and love

The routes reopen to regular traffic

Headlines divulge our darkest moments

In fewer characters than there were on our march

We read them off to one another like bullets

Like knives

Words which slice and fray the edges of

All we tried to build

"Why do we doing it anyway?"

You say; you say

"The come down is harder every year."

Like it was a drug we were on

Meant to manage our brains

"You're going to lose it."

You say it, and I do.

If I am, at the very least, open, it may be possible—
probably probable—to continue.
This—of course—in opposition to a closure (of mind,
of eyes, of sex organs) where I am to be contained.
Done, as it were. Done, as you were, when you
slammed fingers into fists and doors into frames.
Picture me then under glass. Pinned. Wings spread
and pretending pretending pretending to fly.

You pretend (don't we all?) to be enigmatic, like some mystery is just what you needed to be interesting. So I'll pretend (as I do) to be interested. (You like that, don't you? I know I do.) So then we can go on this way, moving in that circular motion of need meeting met meeting want. A false equivalency, really. But we can pretend it's not nearly as easily as we can pretend to desire one another.

You called me once an echo.

"You are not the person I met."

    (Your words, not mine.)

You, the proponent of change and acceptance and

Now something akin to glory in your

"Holier than thou."

    (Your words, now mine.)

Therefore I may only do as you say

"Repeat after me."

Quieter each time. Until I

Fade

Become silent.

Cease.

Cut
To add or subtract
To leave or leave behind
Scars and/or stardust
A singular flare of emotion

That is what they say we are, is it not?
The detritus of space
Of gods or of creation
Transmogrified from mineral to biological and back
again

If true, I am still that change.
I can be that creation.
I will not let it cease just because
You say it bothered one
Whom you did not even know.

Ply me with persimmons. Make me gorge until I am thick with the wetted honey of your fruit. When there is an absence, have me scream for more. Where there is more, leave me in want.

Jelly the remainder. Glass jars in a double boiler. Then—and only then—we see the clear delineation of what is inside and what is out. Screw tight the lid. But not before your knife has sampled the flesh.

And so it is now (isn't it always)
When we find ourselves
In the thick of things.
Boxes stored in closets
Touched only by dust
Over so many years. Ready
(Aren't they always) to divulge.
Time capsules, really,
That wait for us to say
            "That was another time."
            "I was in a different place."
            "Can you believe I ever wore that?"
Pleasantries. Nothing real here.
Even in the thick.

You find a momento. A tiny
Death you want to slip away.
Fold it like a poem on paper.
Only a brief longing (aren't they always)
To keep inside your pocket
For some future attempt
At clarity.

Teach me solace.
How to wrap my mouth around the word
       You were often so good at that. Well-
       Versed in your instruction.
       Demanding.

Show me how the "s" slithers around
The "oh" in a manner so seductive
Even the stoic would blush.

       Require it of them.
       It is their purpose
       Afterall.

Make it long – no, longer still ——
Until it opens so wide your oceans
Will pale into buckets.

Show me how the syllables connect
Like hands brushing one another
In food lines. Both reaching for
The same slice of bread.

Then comes the lace. A veil
Worn on a wedding day.
To a funeral. Both the same in their
Supposed forevers.

"I do not open for just anyone."
You
Say it like you mean it. Like I can't
Count in my head the number
Of our fellows we've both fucked.
You
Speak it like an ancient wisdom.
A tome whose magic is reserved
For only those deemed worthy.

I
Smile,
Believe you.

Each night we call it fury
That which ebbs within us
     and pulls
A haunt quickening our bloodstreams
     until
Each instance of our beings collide
     (another notch in the wall
         from bedposts kept too close)
It really wasn't much of anything, after all.

And then, in collision, in anger, we ride
Until the morning star becomes the sun
     and pulls
The color back to our faces.

We were not truly that at all
     it would seem
The way the day describes the night
     furious
And then subtle, and then still.

We make constellations of our bodies
Stretch out like gods against an unforgiving sky
Make quests of one another
Like this:
       Search. Find. Steal. Once more.
Again and again until the poets can look
Only once and know.

I am not so made for this nihilistic approach
To disbelive the principals of our story
Once each star ceases its glow

For even when your star shot
Trails to distant galaxies, I felt
Within me the reconstitution of heroes:
A villian made holy in the trailing light.

A poet comes along
       Retraces the lines
           Creates new metaphors of
Our story. Says
       There is meaning here.
Writes: I can find none at all.

Paradox

So you can look at the fondness of me
De-romanticized
I take breaths only when you blink
Make sure you never see my chest heave
My jaw clench
The wince within my eyes.

I ensure I am striking
Six : Stand tall like clock hands
Poses : For the family portrait
Myself: Only when your back is turned.

So you can look at your fondness of me
As a reflection of yourself, I hide.
It may be better this way.
You were never one to understand
Nuance.

I am an abomination. You told me as much. With your
1.) Signs at the parade; 2.) Lecture from your pulpit
(Remember? Right before you asked for money–
passing your panhandler's tray; flashing your 900
number across the screen); 3.) Camps; 4.) Denial of
my existance.

Me, the atheist, I detest (though not in the same way
as you) the sense of witnessing against your bile, the
way it carves a river across your tongue, splits it to a
forked seduction.

I approach you like the problem you think I am.
Assign us both the properties of your wisdom.
Provide evidence of your correlation.
Say:

If I=Abomination yet We=Holy, then certainly:

$$\frac{We}{I} = Us = Holy\ Abomination$$

So let it be so. It is written. And we shall take this
unto us as the body and the blood and the wine.

I have done it – exactly what I said I would not. I have pulled the wool over your eyes, dear reader, in as much as I am able to on the arbitrary lines of these pages. You think of me as someone strong, or, at the very least, sure. You read my words, imagine me confident, imagine me kind. You understand the edit, my statements as a filter through how I want to be read, but trust my truthfulness of experience, of rage, of interpretation.

It is this understanding which most intrigues me. This and... whiskey. I want to know how the wool will pull it in. If the fibers may get drunk on it the way you do with my words. Perhaps that is where my confidence lies.

I am terrified. I am enraged. I am numb.

I would say that I'm grieving, except this is not that. The stages of grief are not at play here. There is no denial, no shock. There will certainly be no bargaining. Not with you. Not anymore. And I think we've both assuredly moved far beyond the point of acceptance.

For far too long—years, decades, centuries, all piled atop one another amidst the push and subsequent blowback—queer folks, women, persons of color, persons with disabilities have fought for equality, have struggled to be seen, have asked to simply be allowed to exist.

There's been pushback. Hell, sometimes the push down the stairs comes from inside the house. None of us are blind to that. We've all grown up in the same systems and internalized so many phobias that at times—like you—we have acted unkindly, even toward ourselves. That is not an excuse. It is a call to do the work, to understand the assignment.

I've seen a lot of assertions that the very existence of me is an infringement on your rights. That you should not be forced to accept me. That my and my friends' calls to be equal, to be seen, to exist somehow becomes a gut punch to your very morality.

You've come right out and said it: you will not accept me, accept us. You've been loud and vocal in that response. And, if you haven't, you've let your actions speak for you.

I wish to break this down to its smallest parts. Diagram the sentence simply so that both of us (see how I group you alongside me?) can be very clear on what's being said. So that we both will know why acceptance is no longer on the table. Let's dissect what you are saying when you complain that you are being forced to accept.

You must:
      a) understand that I exist.

Oh, but you shouldn't have to make that acknowledgment, you say. You shouldn't be put out in any way. Your existence should proceed without my involvement. Without my lurking in the peripheral of your mind. Otherwise, I must certainly be forcing you to accept me.

What you are truly saying is:
      "I don't want to have to see you."

A far cry from acceptance, and a short walk to "round 'em up, and ship 'em out."

Now, you may be thinking:
>It's not like that. That's an exaggeration.
>It'll never go that far.

And yet, your actions say otherwise. You've made your voice heard all while attempting to deny me my own, to make me question the warble which escapes my lips as nothing more than breath wasted.

Here's where I stop. Where we stop.

We (here I remove you from the collective) have striven for a common ground, to show you (who has set yourself apart) that we are not too different than you. To present ourself as human in your eyes.

We have reached across the aisle to take your hand, watched it turn away, and yet gladly accept whatever scraps you have offered.
We have turned the other cheek at your comments about the rest of them—"but not you, of course; you're different"—when you've shown us who you are.

Maybe we called you out, or made a little joke, or slowly stopped including you in our lives. Maybe we tried too hard to show you our humanity, to get you to change your mind through the evidence of our being, because we hoped the commonality between us would outweigh the ingrained hatred within you.

Coddle me.
Create a moment from which I do not wish
to emerge.
Give me a reason to be strong enough
                    —finally—
to stop pretending to hold strength.
Teach me the form of hubris possessed
in Incarus so that I may fly
too close to your sun. Or perhaps
in Lucifer so that I may stand up,
refuse to feel my descent as a fall.
Or further still,
in You.
That must be something. To hold
such light you can envelop me,
melt the wax of my ligaments,
watch me plummet and
Smile.

For the sake of this statement:
I will be me and you will be also

There was a moment
Several in fact when
I asked you what it was you
Saw in the clouds. How they
Formed a blanket over the city
In much the way snow will do to
The north.
You cited their softness
The way light could still pass through
The lengths which they would go to
To move.
I sighted their edges
Hard and noticeable
Lined with armor.

(I) twist
Until I have wriggled free, state:
See? This is the proof that:
> A) I have never been held
> B) your grip was always too tight.

I use the undulations of skin, the wavering bits of it
Enticed onward by words,
To note the nuance of your vowels
To set my own apart

It is here that I am wakened
Drawn to quarters by the mercy of the
> A) town — en mass, as only groups are prone
> to marches
> B) town's crier — his words a mimic of what
> he was told, foregoing truth to
> appease those who line his coffers,
> dealing blows from both sides:
>> 1) headlines
>>> shifted toward power
>> 2) paywalls
>>> angled toward rage
> C) cryer — salt an accusation still rooted in
> your palm; along the curve of your
> twisted cheek.

To be clear, I am not advocating violence.
Though it is not off the table.

Like shall be met with like after all.
The first brick at stonewall
was a response to the baton. You threw
the first stone.

I am no longer playing nice.
I am no longer allowing myself to simply exist
within your structures. I remove myself
from them, from you. I will not do
the work within the parameters you have set
and allow you to reap the benefits of my struggle.

If I wasn't so scared I'd be laughing.

Anyone, when given to a particularity of circumstance, may become....

A genius.

And that's what I was. A tried and true genius.

A villain.

If there is to be a sickle, for indeed the must be, I pray the blade be not dull. You know I am not one for praying, so you pay no mind as you prey.

When you arrive—the jester; the actor—I will gather stones. Wet them. Push them to metal to sharpen your scythe. Wait. Wait. Wait for you to make the first slice. Indulge the cut as painful, the reaction you were hoping for, and pretend I understand the script inscribed there on the stem.

It is your play, after all: the role you were born for. I roll with the dialogue, the punches of your emphatic punctations. Ignore the stage directions, suggestions as they are, and take me down before act three.

I wait. Squander moments like
the details you remove from your re-telling of us.
Cut at the edges—split ends and nails first;
the bits that seem less than natural—until
the whole of who I am becomes
suruptciously pellucid.
It is then and only then
when I may know who I am.
It is your design of me which allows
who I was to be freed. A sense of becoming
in the aftermath: the sputtered fray of
blame to make me whole.

I am an impish being
Cut
From the trunk of an oak tree
Extricated from that which holds the earth together
A solemn promise that was really a necessity

How else would I repurpose your energy
Take it inside to throw it back to you
Become one with what you deemed offensive
Expelled
Augment it into beauty (how glorious)
To give breath to my words

Wade in. Disturb the water just so—rings which echo out; chains around your feet—until you are ankle deep in sin. There, learn to relish the sensation of what could never be yours.

Minnows will nibble at your skin, leave behind puckering reminders of what it means to be annointed.

Too, hares will taunt you from the shore. Claim virtue in their dryness. Demand you wallow; demand you drown. (Their grace could never match your own.)

When the water stills once more, feel the bonds set. Call them solid where you have displaced them. Call them a measure in entropy. Let them be both at once, everything. Nothing.

I have found (as if it was lost) a commonality amongst the fondest of my emotions. I love with a like passion to my rage. Burn down encyclopedias. Let knowledge wither on the vine. Turn two eyes down to the antelope sky.

I have lost (as if it was found) any presumption to posterity (the pre-position of). I let it slip from my skin like sweat, drenched on the too-worn day. Soak the concrete slab of foundations until the carrion peck the remnants. Place palms upon persimmons. Offer them to passers-by.

I have finished what was never started in dreams, the sweet-meat fruits of nomadic animals. No rest. No roost. Only more work to be done.

I make peonies of paper
Wire stems and dabs of glue
Arrange them just so
State: these, like my care, shall never wilt.

Thousands of petals, edged in claws
Retractable cuts beneath bandages
Add color once they've dried.
A statement vase. A bouquet.

I watch you place them on the coffee table
Tilt them toward the slip
Of light from behind the curtains
Smile.

One day, absent-minded,
You will water them.
Watch the paper curl
Disintegrate.

And again at midnight I race through the obstacle course of expressions, face fierce and armored, chainmail clinking on bone. Think of it as a mask— why should one be burdened with fact?—I am merely trying on. Clang against the mirror; see if glass is as deserving as you were once meant to be.

When we were younger, which could have been any moment before now, indeed any time after this one, I had the ability to dazzle when my impudence was turned elsewhere. It is only recently when I have turned it upon myself. Or, perhaps, in only this moment. But, you see, I have no choice.

I am friends with Orpheus. An acquaintance really. Friend being to solid a word for the intimate knowledge I possess and he disposes of. Yet he did once warn me of the dangers of looking back in darkness.

The mirror, though. O, the mirror! I musn't turn to see behind. Simply study—tics, curves, blemishes— until you appear.

If I were to:
                dance   my
                        limbs   akimbo
        leaves on an   autumn   breeze
Would you believe me joyful?
                A thing to be cut from the world.
Studied.   Calcified.   Hardened.

Say: How dare your mirth whistle where mine
                may only hum.

Demand answers in the only words you understand.

Stand still.   Scowl.   Watch
                                                                rhythm
                                                reach
                        backwards
            in
Time.

Preposterous, really, you say. The notion of moonlight
when we know it merely a reflection of the sun.

I smile a waning grin. Take your words.
Make them something new.
Give them back to you.

The wound has been cauterized—another sore within itself, but at least it no longer bleeds. In time, it will harden; scar. Form its solid mass upon my skin to remind me of the slices you took when I wasn't looking. I will garnish it with rosemary salves, garlic, thyme, and the occasional dandelion. Make a feast of the memory. Say it no longer hurts until you are thirsty, once more, for blood.

Beneath the privet, still plunged into the pot, we have a pride flag. Progressive is what they call it. A memory of three, no, four years ago now. Bedraggled by soil pushed upwards in rainfall. It still waves when the wind blows just so.

Bees are attracted to its colors. And wasps. Alight. Expect nectar. Then move on to the hellebores.

Its pot cannot be moved. I believe the roots of the shrub have filled the drainage holes, spread from the potting soil to the red clay beneath. Spread. Attempted to slow the rotation of the earth.

One day they will reach for our bodies—neither of us want coffins, you see. They will find what is left of us, the last of us. Use what we were to break the confines of the ceramic until the flag is no longer contained.

You, the unknowable god that you are, preen against a backdrop of azure. Let moss tickle your feet. Bathe in the petals of apple blossoms, those lost to breeze before they could wither, turn to fruit.

Be still.
Breath in measures of song
(Quick! Pull the ruler out!)
Keep time in the rise and fall
Of your chest.
It is a hard thing
This new wall around you.
Firm in form with
One brick stacked atop the other
Mortar between mortality
A whistle though. A tiny gasp of air.
A small cut caused by settled
(That of others; surely not of yourself)
Listen to the song it makes
Let it guide you
When to strike.

Leaves begin to unfurl
Puckered against stems
Like aphids clawing at what waits inside
Yet the blooms of last fall have gone gray or brown
Parched yet holding shape.
You deadhead them
Let them fall beneath the shrub
Promise them back to the earth
I smile. Tell you: a job well-done
You shrug. The pruning sheers did
The bulk of the work.

We walk the grounds in
The early afternoon, hands on
Hips or
One crossed into the crook of arms
The other under chins
Point, say: how 'bout here?
Study the terrain
Slant eyes toward sky
Look to rooflines of the nearby buildings
Say: six hours of morning sun
Should be enough
Spread new soil and remove rocks
Wait for seeds to root.

Tomorrow we will clean out closets packed
From when we moved in
Check to see if anything has grown.

When we were new we were insatiable
Dipped lavender into honeyed pots
Swam streets with arms locked
Laughed in unison at inappropriate times
Sat together on a single booth in restaurants

Now a chasm forms
A procurement of space needed to house a past
TV dinners in laps
And empty cushion on the couch between

And yet I know the string that connects us
Has not been cut
Threadbare though it may be

I know a time will come when
We must once again lock arms
Even as the guise of age makes us lean
In order to walk, to keep aloft

When I say I cannot wait
To grow old together
What I mean is I miss
The omnipresence of your touch

If I am to guide you back, offer directions from spaces I have never been, I must rely first upon your truth. Tell me, what is that you see? Describe, in detail, the way the moss has grown on my body. Make believe that old scouting trick was true: that it will always face north in this hemisphere. We may then determine which direction I was facing when you first turned your back. From there, we may find our way home.

There it is
The cut you promised you would make
Smaller than I'd imagined it would be

Keep it open
Keep it open
Keep it open

From it, let the honey
Flow.

Claude Moore is a pseudonym. Claude Moore is an idea. Is a poet. Is an amalgamation. Claude Moore is a container—like a book in that way— broken open. Claude Moore uses they/them pronouns in respect of their namesakes who did not have that language, yet provided every nuance to the words.

This is their second book of poetry.

Founded in Atlanta, Georgia in 2023, PARLYAREE PRESS is dedicated to publishing writing that expands, reveals, and interrogates the mainstream. We seek out fiction, creative nonfiction, and poetry that exists in the liminal space between what was and what will be.

The cant of circus performers, freaks, queers, and thespians, Parlyaree is the invented language required to tell the stories of those othered, to keep their secrets, to keep them safe. It is a polyglot of experiences that may only be told in one's own voice. Parlyaree—as an invented language—borrows from what was to create something new.

That is what excites us at Parlyaree Press. Stories that transform; essays that reimagine; poetry that takes us behind the stanza to the core of our being and back again; language that plays as much as it conveys.

Writers: tell us your secrets.
Readers: reimagine your worlds.

www.ingramcontent.com/pod-product-compliance
Lightning Source LLC
Chambersburg PA
CBHW012051150626
46549CB00023B/3229